Anders Lustg

Lampedusa

Bloomsbury Methuen Drama
An imprint of Bloomsbury Publishing Plc

B L O O M S B U R Y
LONDON · OXFORD · NEW YORK · NEW DELHI · SYDNEY

Bloomsbury Methuen Drama

An imprint of Bloomsbury Publishing Plc

Imprint previously known as Methuen Drama

50 Bedford Square   1385 Broadway
London   New York
WC1B 3DP   NY 10018
UK   USA

www.bloomsbury.com

**BLOOMSBURY, METHUEN DRAMA and the Diana logo
are trademarks of Bloomsbury Publishing Plc**

First published 2015
Reprinted by Bloomsbury Methuen Drama 2015

British Library Cataloguing-in-Publication Data
A catalogue record for this book is available from the British Library.

ISBN: PB: 978-1-4742-5355-0
ePub: 978-1-4742-5356-7
ePDF: 978-1-4742-5357-4

Library of Congress Cataloging-in-Publication Data
A catalog record for this book is available from the Library of Congress.

Series: Modern Plays

Typeset by Mark Heslington Ltd, Scarborough, North Yorkshire
Printed and bound in Great Britain

Introduction

This will never stop.

Last year 170,100 refugees reached Italian shores by boat from Africa. That's a rise of over 300% on the 42,925 people who arrived in 2013. They used to come only in the calmer summer months, but now they brave the winter storms and twenty foot waves too. The numbers for the first two months of 2015 are double those for 2014.

This is not a blip. An aberration. These people will never stop coming. However many of them we try to drown or lock up.

In an act of moral cowardice unusually repugnant even by British standards, our government led the way in ending Mare Nostrum, the EU's rescue operation in the Mediterranean, last year, at the exact time when the need for it became extreme. More than 4,000 refugees drowned in the Med in 2014 despite Mare Nostrum (the real figure is much higher—those are only the bodies that were recovered). How many will die now it's been withdrawn?

The replacement program, Triton, has a third of the resources and is limited to patrolling within thirty miles of the Italian coast. This amounts to an official policy of deliberately letting migrants drown to deter others from coming, cloaked under a nauseating faux-concern for their well-being.

Europe's other proposed responses are equally barbaric. Militarised camps, aka 'processing centres', on the southern shores of the Med. Arming the navies of Maghreb countries to intercept the migrant boats, round them up and send them back where they came from. 'This would produce a real deterrent effect, so that fewer and fewer migrants would be ready to put their life at risk to reach European coasts,' as the leaked Italian proposal for the latter scheme put it.

Except it wouldn't. At the heart of our self-delusion about migration is a wilful misunderstanding of why people come. They don't come to soak the benefits system, because hardly any of them know it exists. They come out of desperation, because their country is on fire or their government is repressive or climate change is killing their crops. Often that's down to the West. We removed the Gaddafi regime in Libya, odious as it might have been, leaving a vacuum state that's the epicentre of migrant smuggling. We are right behind the Sisi regime in Egypt, which is cracking down on Arab Spring dissidents and Muslims. Sisi is also privatising state assets at a rate of knots (which is a key reason why the West supports him), putting large numbers of workers on the street. There's a long and intimate connection between World Bank privatisation schemes and mass migration. We're the primary source of climate change emissions. I don't need to tell you what we've done in the Middle East.

We urgently need a proper conversation about migration in this country, and in Europe. To acknowledge what we do to *cause* migration and correct it. To decide what we're going to do about our rapidly aging population, which requires an infusion of hundreds of thousands of young, talented, hard-working people to keep up the employment base. Who wins and who loses if we let those people in? What about the extra load on public services? Does that require a major increase in taxation of the rich? (Spoiler: of course it fucking does.) What about the morality of taking skilled people from poor countries who need them even more than we do? What do contemporary patterns of outsourcing and de-skilling in many professions imply for our future needs?

The basic question we need to ask ourselves, and without giving too much away this underscores both storylines, is what kind of society do we want to be?

We don't have any of these conversations. Instead, we just let people drown.

That is pure cowardice. All my plays are about bringing the reality of what's really happening in the world home, and that's what happens to both characters in this play. They keep the reality of what they do at arm's length, until one day they just can't any more. The barrier cracks. What will they do then?

I hope our collective barrier cracks, and soon. And when it does, that we will have the courage and the dignity to ask the right questions.

Anders Lustgarten
20 March 2015

Acknowledgements

Big thanks to Steven Atkinson, Holly Kendrick and all at HighTide, Nina Steiger, David Luff and all at Soho Theatre, Rod Dixon at Red Ladder, Matthew Linley at Unity, David Mercatali, Ben Monks and Will Young, and Christopher Eccleston.

I'd been planning to write something on Lampedusa for years but wasn't sure how to convey the vastness of scale till I saw Grounded, and particularly its star Lucy Ellinson. So thanks to her too.

And the usual thanks to Ange and Joseph, the Old Skooler, Mum and Chris, and Beeper Beeper that Featured Creature (plus pingouin). Lots of love.

This play is dedicated to the people who didn't make it.

Anders Lustgarten

Acknowledgements

HIGHTIDE FESTIVAL THEATRE AND SOHO THEATRE IN ASSOCIATION WITH UNITY THEATRE LIVERPOOL PRESENT

LAMPEDUSA

A world premiere by Anders Lustgarten

Lampedusa was first performed at Soho Theatre, London, on Wednesday 8th April 2014.

The production then transferred to the 2015 HighTide Festival, Aldeburgh, Suffolk, on Thursday 10th September 2015 and Unity Theatre, Liverpool, on Thursday 24th September 2015.

Supported using public funding by
ARTS COUNCIL ENGLAND
LOTTERY FUNDED

Lampedusa

by

Anders Lustgarten

A HighTide Festival Theatre and Soho Theatre co-production

Stefano	**Ferdy Roberts**
Denise	**Louise Mai Newberry**

CREATIVE TEAM

Director	**Steven Atkinson**
Designer	**Lucy Osborne**
Lighting Designer	**Elliot Griggs**
Sound Designer	**Isobel Waller-Bridge**
Assistant Director	**Rosy Banham**
Casting Director	**Nadine Rennie CDG**
Dramaturg	**Nina Steiger**
Associate Designer	**James Turner**
Costume Supervisor	**Natasha Ward**
Production Manager	**Cath Bates**
Stage Manager	**Julia Nimmo**
Assistant Stage Manager	**Andrew McCabe**

With thanks to:

Justin Audibert, Richard Beecham, Christopher Eccleston, Michael
Fentiman, Rob Hastie, Robert Icke, Prasanna Puwanarajah

Cast

Louise Mai Newberry (Denise)

Louise Mai trained at East 15 and Cambridge University (when full grants still existed).

Theatre includes: *Battersea Stories* (Lightbox Theatre); *The Long Life & Great Good Fortune of John Clare* (Eastern Angles); *Pericles, Two Gentlemen of Verona* (Factory); *Pick-Ups, Sacred Nymphs of Natterjack* (Bush Theatre); *Adventures in Wonderland, Twelfth Night* (Teatro Vivo); *wAve, Boom, Dim Sum Nights* (Yellow Earth); *The Gruffalo, The Snow Dragon* (Tall Stories); *Not the End of the World* (Bristol Old Vic); *Transmissions* (Birmingham Rep); *Good Woman of Setzuan* (Leicester Haymarket); *Noah's Ark* (Walk the Plank); *King Lear* (Orange Tree); *The Lion, The Witch and The Wardrobe* (RSC).

Television and film includes: *Doctors, The Bill, Goal!, Dream Machines, Futuremakers, Fluid, Fracking Regent's Park, Nydenion, Christie, The God Game, Tsuppari*.

She writes and performs as the comedy character 'Precious Jade'.

Ferdy Roberts (Stefano)

Ferdy is co-Artistic Director of Filter Theatre and an Associate Artist of the Lyric, Hammersmith.

Theatre for Filter: *Macbeth, A Midsummer Night's Dream, Three Sisters* (Lyric Hammersmith); *Water* (Lyric/BAM, New York); *Twelfth Night* (Tricycle); *The Caucasian Chalk Circle* (National Theatre); *Faster* (London/New York).

Other theatre: *Shakespeare in Love* (West End); *Open Court, If You Don't Let Us Dream, We Won't Let You Sleep* (Royal Court); *Three Kingdoms* (Lyric/Munich Kammerspiel/Teater NO99); *Wallenstein* (Chichester); *The Birthday Party, The Dumb Waiter* (Bristol Old Vic); *Frankenstein* (Derby Playhouse); *Another Country* (West End); *The Changeling, Beautiful Thing* (Salisbury Playhouse).

Television includes: *Foyle's War, Whistleblower, The Bill, Goldplated, Your Mother Should Know, Holby City*.

Film includes: *What You Will, Mr Nice, Sex & Drugs & Rock & Roll*.

Company

Anders Lustgarten (Writer)

Anders Lustgarten won the inaugural Harold Pinter Playwright's Award for *If You Don't Let Us Dream ,We Won't Let You Sleep* at the Royal Court Theatre Downstairs. He is currently under commission to the Royal Court and the National Theatre among several others, and is also adapting David Peace's *The Damned United* for a national stage tour. He's also a long-standing political activist who's been arrested in four continents.

Steven Atkinson (Director)

For HighTide: *Lampedusa* (Soho Theatre/HighTide Festival); *peddling* (Arcola Theatre/Off-Broadway/HighTide Festival); *Pussy Riot: Hunger Strike* (Bush Theatre/Southbank Centre); *Neighbors* (Nuffield Theatre/HighTide Festival); *Bottleneck* (Soho Theatre/UK tour); *Clockwork* (HighTide Festival); *Bethany* (HighTide Festival/Public Theater, New York); *Incoming* (Latitude Festival/HighTide Festival); *Dusk Rings a Bell* (Watford Palace Theatre/HighTide Festival); *Lidless* (Trafalgar Studios/HighTide Festival); *Muhmah* (HighTide Festival), and *The Pitch* (Latitude Festival).

Other direction includes: *Three Card Trick* (Liverpool Everyman and Playhouse); *The Afghan and the Penguin* (BBC Radio 4); *Freedom Trilogy* (Hull Truck Theatre); *Sexual Perversity in Chicago* (Edinburgh Festival).

Awards: Fringe First Awards for *Educating Ronnie* and *Lidless*; two SOLT Stage One Bursaries for *Lidless* and *Stovepipe*; 2009 Whatsonstage Award nomination for Best Off-West End Production for *Stovepipe*; Esquire's Brilliant Brits 2009.

Steven co-founded HighTide Festival Theatre and is its Artistic Director. He read Film and Theatre at Reading University, graduating in 2005.

Lucy Osborne (Designer)

Theatre includes: *Privacy, Coriolanus, Berenice* and *The Recruiting Officer* (Donmar Warehouse); *Translations* (UK Theatre Awards Best Touring Production 2014, ETT, Sheffield Theatres, Rose Kingston); *Hello/Goodbye, In the Vale of Health, Blue Heart Afternoon* (Hampstead); *Plenty, The Unthinkable, The Machine* (Manchester International Festival/NYC); *The Long and the Short and the Tall* (Sheffield Lyceum Theatre); *Huis Clos* (Donmar Trafalgar Season); *Twelfth Night* (Winner of the Chicago Jeff Award for Scenic Design); *The Taming of the Shrew* (Chicago Shakespeare Theatre); *Shades* (Royal Court).

Lucy is the co-designer of *Roundabout*, a portable theatre which won The Stage Awards 'Theatre Building of the Year 2015'. Her work for Paines Plough includes: *The Angry Brigade* (Bush Theatre), *An Intervention* (Watford Palace/UK tour); *Jumpers for Goalposts* (Hull Truck, Watford Palace and Bush Theatre); the *Roundabout Seasons* (2011, 2012 and 2014) and *Love, Love, Love* (Royal Court/national tour).

Elliot Griggs (Lighting Designer)

Theatre includes: *Benefit* (Cardboard Citizens); *Yen* (Manchester Royal Exchange); *Pomona* (Orange Tree Theatre); *Fleabag* (Soho Theatre/UK tour); *Henry IV* (Associate Lighting Designer, Donmar Warehouse), *CommonWealth* (Almeida Theatre); *He Had Hairy Hands, The Boy Who Kicked Pigs* (The Lowry, Manchester/UK tour); *Bitter Pleasures for a Sour Generation* (Soho Theatre); *Marching On Together* (Old Red Lion); *Rachel, John Ferguson, Spokesong* (Finborough Theatre).

Awards: Best Lighting Designer (Off West End Awards 2014); New Talent in Entertainment Lighting (ALD 2014); Francis Reid Award (ALD 2011); ShowLight Award (NSDF 2009).

Training: RADA.

Isobel Waller-Bridge (Sound Designer)

For HighTide: *Incognito* (HighTide Festival/Bush Theatre – winner of the 2015 Off West End Award for Best Sound Design*)*.

Other theatre includes: *Posh* (Nottingham Playhouse/Salisbury Arts Theatre); *Exit the King* (Bath Theatre Royal); *Uncle Vanya* (St James Theatre/Jagged Fence); *Billy Liar* (Manchester Royal Exchange); *Not the Worst Place* (Sherman Cymru); *Yellow Face* (National Theatre, NTShed); *Fleabag* (Soho Theatre); *Orlando* (Manchester Royal Exchange); *The Ideal World Season* (Watford Palace Theatre); *Forever House* (Theatre Royal Plymouth); *Sleuth* (The Watermill).

As composer: *Hope Place* (Liverpool Everyman); *King Lear* (Chichester Festival Theatre); *Neville's Island* (Chichester Festival Theatre/Duke of York's); *If Only* (Minerva Theatre).

Rosy Banham (Assistant Director)

Directing includes: *The Pier* (Marlowe Studio/Burton Taylor Studio, Oxford Playhouse); *Mush and Me* (Bush Theatre/JW3/Edinburgh Fringe/Adelaide Fringe); *England Street, If You're Glad I'll Be Frank* (Burton Taylor Studio, Oxford Playhouse); *Edges* (Edinburgh Fringe); *Charity Begins at Home* (Waterloo East).

Assistant directing includes: *Things We Do For Love* (Theatre Royal Bath/UK tour); *Bracken Moor* (Tricycle); *NSFW, The Witness* (Royal Court); *A Kind of Alaska, Krapp's Last Tape, Coasting* (Bristol Old Vic); *Dick Whittington* (Oxford Playhouse); *The Comedy of Errors* (Tobacco Factory).

HighTide Festival Theatre

"That powerhouse of new writing" The Observer

"Famous for championing emerging playwrights and contemporary theatre"
Daily Mail

HighTide Festival Theatre is one of the UK's leading producers of new plays, and the only professional theatre focused on the production of new playwrights. Currently we read and consider around 1000 scripts a year from around the world, from which we then work with 100 playwrights on a range of development opportunities, from workshops to full productions. Every play that we receive is read by our Artistic Director and Associates.

Under Steven Atkinson, co-founding Artistic Director, we have premièred major productions by playwrights including Ella Hickson, Frances Ya-Chu Cowhig, Nick Payne, Adam Brace, Beth Steel, Sam Holcroft, Luke Barnes, Vickie Donoghue, Lydia Adetunji, Jack Thorne and Joel Horwood. We produce several productions a year in our annual Suffolk festival and on tour.

In eight years we have staged over fifty productions, producing new work with some of the world's leading theatres in London (including the National Theatre, Bush Theatre, Old Vic Theatre and Soho Theatre), regionally (including Sheffield Theatres, Watford Palace and Theatre Royal Bath) and internationally (in Off Broadway, 59E59, New York City and the Public Theater, and in Australia the National Play Festival).

Lansons host our administrative offices in-kind within their Clerkenwell offices. This innovative partnership between a business and charity has won five Corporate Engagement Awards, a Social Impact Award, two Arts & Business award nominations, and has been profiled by the Guardian and the Evening Standard.

HighTide Festival Theatre is a National Portfolio Organisation of Arts Council England.

HT
2015

Our 2015 Season will commence with the transfer of Vinay Patel's *True Brits* to London's Vault Festival, co-produced with Rich Mason Productions, following runs at the Bush Theatre and Edinburgh Festival.

Harry Melling's *peddling* will premiere in London at the Arcola Theatre following an acclaimed opening at the 2014 HighTide Festival and off-Broadway run.

Anders Lustgarten's new play *Lampedusa* will premiere at the Soho Theatre in April and later transfer to the 2015 HighTide Festival. This HighTide and Soho Theatre co-production is directed by Steven Atkinson.

In September the 2015 HighTide Festival will take place in Aldeburgh, Suffolk. In addition to *Lampedusa*, we will produce the world premiere of three more productions, alongside a full festival programme of talks, play readings and touring productions.

For full details please visit www.hightide.org.uk

Image: *Incognito* by Nick Payne (HighTide 2014)
Photographer: Bill Knight

Charitable Support

HighTide is a registered charity (1124477) and we are grateful to the many organisations and individuals who support our work, enabling us to keep our ticket prices low and accessible to many different audiences around the world.

There are very talented young playwrights working in the UK, and if they are lucky they will find their way to the HighTide Festival Theatre season in Suffolk. I hope you will join me in supporting this remarkable and modest organisation. With your help HighTide can play an even more major role in promoting the best of new writing in the UK.

Lady Susie Sainsbury

HighTide Festival Theatre is a National Portfolio Organisation of Arts Council England.

Major Supporters

Arts Council England, Lansons, Old Possum's Practical Trust, The Backstage Trust, The Garfield Weston Foundation, IdeasTap.

Corporate Supporters

John Clayton and Bishops Printers, CMS Cameron McKenna, Northern Trust.

Individual Supporters

Clare Parsons and Tony Langham, Criona Palmer and Tony Mackintosh, Albert and Marjorie Scardino, Peter Wilson MBE.

Trusts and Foundations

Adnams Charity, Britten-Pears Foundation, Goldsmiths' Company Charity, Fidelio Charitable Trust, Foyle Foundation, Golsoncott Foundation, Leche Trust, The Mackintosh Foundation, Martin Bowley Charitable Trust, The Parham Trust, Ronald Duncan Literary Foundation, Scarfe Charitable Trust.

With thanks to Shoreditch Town Hall and all our Friends of the Festival and Host Families.

How to Support HighTide

If you are interested in supporting our work, please contact Freddie Porter on 0207 566 9765 or email freddie@hightide.org.uk

Media Partners

Artistic Development

Send us your play

At HighTide we pride ourselves on discovering new playwrights and giving their play a world-class production. If you are a playwright looking for your big-break, then we want to read the best unproduced play you have.

We accept scripts from around the world via our website. Scripts are read by our Artistic Director and Artistic Associates. Of the 1000 scripts we receive annually, 100 writers are then invited to work with the company through workshops, readings, and full productions.

Our submission window is open twice a year. To submit a play please visit: *www.hightide.org.uk/playwriting*

Writers on Attachment

Our Writers on Attachment programme is a talent development initiative that is supported by Arts Council England South East through Grants for the Arts.

The scheme is designed to support early career playwrights from the South East of England, and those wanting to work in the region to develop their work and showcase their work at partner theatres, who have included Eastern Angles, Mercury Theatre Colchester and Watford Palace Theatre.

As part of a writers' group, six writers each year are offered a bespoke package of development including support in writing, fundraising and producing, and HighTide connects each of the group to the wider theatre industry. The attachment includes access to one-on-one sessions, workshops, time with creatives and other writers and may lead to work being shared or fully produced in the future.

Applications for the 2015/16 Escalator Plays intake open in Summer 2015. For more information see *www.hightide.org.uk/attachment_ programme*

For more information about working with HighTide please contact Stephanie Street, Literary Associate: *stephanie@hightide.org.uk*

LONDON'S MOST VIBRANT VENUE FOR NEW THEATRE, COMEDY AND CABARET

Soho Theatre is a major creator of new theatre, comedy and cabaret. Across our three different spaces we curate the finest live performance we can discover, develop and nurture. Soho Theatre works with theatre makers and companies in a variety of ways, from full producing of new plays, to co-producing new work, working with associate artists and presenting the best new emerging theatre companies that we can find.

We have numerous writers and theatre makers on attachment and under commission, six young writers and comedy groups and we read and see hundreds of shows a year – all in an effort to bring our audience work that amazes, moves and inspires.

**'Soho Theatre was buzzing, and there were queues all over the building as audiences waited to go into one or other of the venue's spaces. [The audience] is so young, exuberant and clearly anticipating a good time.'
Guardian**

We attract over 170,000 audience members a year. We produced, co-produced or staged over forty new plays in the last twelve months.

Our social enterprise business model means that we maximise value from Arts Council and philanthropic funding; we actually contribute more to government in tax and NI than we receive in public funding.

sohotheatre.com

Keep up to date:
sohotheatre.com/mailing-list
facebook.com/sohotheatre
twitter.com/sohotheatre
youtube.com/sohotheatre

Registered Charity No: 267234

Soho Theatre, 21 Dean Street
London W1D 3NE
Admin 020 7287 5060
Box Office 020 7478 0100

Supported using public funding by
ARTS COUNCIL ENGLAND
LOTTERY FUNDED

SUBMITTING YOUR WORK TO SOHO THEATRE

We make the very best entertaining, challenging, profound new work across a range of live performance genres.

We are the place where emerging and established writers conceive, develop and realise their work.

We want to push the form in a way that delights and inspires our audience.

There are no thematic, political or philosophical constraints and though we love to produce a writers' first play, we have no objection to your second, third or fiftieth.

We are looking for work that:
- **Can move people to laugh, cry, argue, protest, celebrate and act**
- **Resonates in the world today**
- **Is inherently theatrical and live**
- **Is risk-taking, brave and visionary**

If you would like to submit a script to us please send it as a PDF or Word attachment to **submissions@sohotheatre.com**.

Your play will go directly to our Artistic team.

We consider every submission for production or for further development opportunities. Although there are a limited number of slots on our stages, we engage with writers throughout the year through workshops, readings, notes sessions and other opportunities.

THE VERITY BARGATE AWARD 2015

We will shortly be announcing the Launch of the 2015 Verity Bargate Award.

The prize was established in 1982 to honour Soho Theatre's co-founder and is presented biennially to an artist resident in the British Isles and Republic of Ireland with fewer than three professional productions.

Past VBA winners include: Vicky Jones, Thomas Eccleshare, Insook Chappell, Matt Charman, Shan Khan, Bonnie Greer, Toby Whithouse and Diane Samuels.

We will be visiting several partner companies around the UK offering information sessions and workshops for writers, as well as a schedule of events throughout the Spring and Summer at Soho Theatre. Full details will be released soon.

2013 winner, *The One* by Vicky Jones, premeiered at Soho Theatre in February 2014, directed by Steve Marmion.

unitytheatre

Unity Theatre, Liverpool

Unity Theatre is Liverpool's radical small-scale theatre with big ambitions. Under the leadership of new Artistic Director, Matthew Linley (and before him long-standing Artistic Director emeritus, Graeme Phillips) their programme of presented and produced work is edgy, radical and unashamedly contemporary, while their talent development programmes have aided the establishment of many of the UK's top touring companies including Told by an Idiot, Ad Infinitum and Kaboodle productions. Recent successes have included productions of Chris Chibnall's *Gaffer*, Bruce Norris' *Clybourne Park* and an international touring production of David Yip's *Gold Mountain*.

unitytheatreliverpool.co.uk

Chair	Chris Bliss
Board	Kirsty Connell, Ali Harwood, Catrina Hewitson, Chris Hulme, Nick Orr and Richard Morgan
Artistic Director and Chief Executive	Matthew Linley
Artistic Director Emeritus	Graeme Phillips
Executive Director	Sue Williams
Technical Manager	Phil Saunders
Marketing Manager	Sam Freeman
Participation Manager	Louise Flooks
House Manager	Chris Hennessey
Financial Officer	Alan Matthews
Technical Assistant	Julie Kearney
Box Office Co-ordinator	Lisa Buckby
Marketing Assistant	Paul Dunbar
Administrative Assistant	Annemarie Martin
Assistant House Manager	Annette Kaviani

Unity Theatre, Liverpool, gratefully acknowledges the support of its funders

  it's liverpool

A private company limited by guarantee number 3333987 / Registered charity number 1062 463

Lampedusa

by Anders Lustgarten

Spotlight on **Stefano**, *alone, reflective. A cigarette burns in his hand. He stares out into the great wide expanse of the Mediterranean Sea.*

Pause. He takes a long drag, then speaks.

Stefano   This is where the world began. This was Caesar's highway. Hannibal's road to glory. These were the trading routes of the Phoenicians and the Carthaginians, the Ottomans and the Byzantines. If you look carefully, my grandfather used to say, you can still make out the wakes of their ships. Our favourite food is *bottarga*, salted roe: it tastes like being slapped in the face by a wave you didn't see coming. We all come from the sea and back to the sea we will go. The Mediterranean gave birth to the world.

On a clear day I am Caesar. The prow of the boat cuts the horizon in two. Sunlight shatters off the waves. Dolphins. Great flocks of seabirds. The ocean sucks and pulses like a giant lung, breathing life into the world even as the wind pushes the air from my lungs and makes it hard to breathe. I forget this is a job. I forget why I am here, except to be alive.

And then I see. And I remember why.

The lung has little black spots floating on its surface. Distant. Hardly visible in the light.

The boat gets closer.
Salvatore cuts the engine.
We drift alongside . . .

Beat.

The bodies of the drowned are more varied than you'd think. Some are warped, rotted, bloated to three times their natural size, twisted into fantastical and disgusting shapes like the curse in that story my grandmother used to tell me. Dead of winter, chills down yer spine.

Others are calm, no signs of struggle, as if they're dozing in the sun on a lazy summer afternoon and a tap on the arm will bring them gently awake. Those are the hardest. Because they're the most human.

They're overwhelmingly young, the dead. Twenties. Thirty at most.
Kids, a lot of them.
You have to be to make the journey, I suppose.

It feels very strange to see so many young people dead. Unnatural.

Everybody tries, at one time or another, to wake the ones that still look human.
A pinch. A splash of water on the face.
'Come on, get up.'

Beat.

The state of a drowned corpse depends on several factors.
How long it's been in the water.
Temperature.
Tides. If the tides bring colder water up from the depths, bodies can be preserved more or less intact for a surprisingly long time.

That has two consequences. One is that although the cold water preserves the bodies, it also alters the make-up of human flesh. Physically, chemically, whatever, I don't know exactly, but . . .
They fall apart in your hands. If they've been in the drink a while. Slide apart and fall to pieces. The sensation is like . . . like oiled lumpy rubbish bags sliding through your fingers.

The other is that colder water brings more fish. The drowned lie facedown, heads lolling down into the water, and fish go for the easiest parts to reach.

Eyelids.
Pieces of the face.
Fingertips.
Anything not protected by clothing, basically.

The bulging eyes of the dead. That's how you know they're gone.

The shock, the sheer horror, wears off eventually, but the sense of dread as we pull up, of not knowing what we're going to find? That never goes away.

Lights down on Stefano. Lights up on **Denise***, mixed white and East Asian, cautious, observant. She watches us. Beat.*

Denise There's all kinds of reactions. There's the ones who act like it's nowt. 'Can you come back later, love? I'm watching the telly.' 'A television means you have assets and therefore means of repayment, am I correct in that, sir?' They look at you different then. There's them who pretend not to understand English, so we have to use sign language. (*She rubs her fingers together and holds out a hand.*) There's the ones who do a flit. I had a bloke jump out t'window on me the other day, not sure he remembered he were on the third floor. Broke his ankle in two places. When I caught up with him, hobbling across the car park, he goes, 'Oh, there you are, love. Left me cheque book in the car.'

And then there's the creative ones. Generally I find the madder the excuses, the more likely they are to be true. Today I had, 'I can't deal with this now, me python's just eaten me dog.' Went in after the bloke and fuck me if there isn't a *massive* snake lying across the carpet, in a right food coma, and bang in his middle is a dog-shaped bulge so tight you can actually make out the curls of the poor bugger's fur. 'That's a miniature Schnauzer, ent it?' I said to him. 'Lovely dogs. Full of energy.' He went *mad*.

All kinds of reactions.
But the overriding one is people do not take it seriously.
As if it's not really happening.
Not here. To them. Now.

People are strange.
When you're a stranger.

Beat.

It's a myth that we send the heavies round at the drop of a hat. There's a range of options available to us. First of all we put what's called a CPA, a Continuous Payment Authority, on the bank account. That gives us the right to access income streams ahead of other claimants, rent and such. After that it's calls to the house, to the employer (should there be one), letters. When none of that works, a more direct approach is required. That is where I come in.

The company prefers to send a woman. They think it leads to less violence. Two flaws with that theory. One is that men do not like to be embarrassed by a woman, and they particularly don't like being asked for money. It hurts their pride. So there are incidents.

The other is that half our customers are women. And the dirty little secret of women is women fucking hate each other. I've never been afraid collecting off a man, but I dread dealing with a woman.
Nails down yer cheek.
Spitting.
The nastiest, most malicious abuse about me race, me face, me body.

They judge me doing this job the way they'd *never* judge a man. Like I've violated some code of 'solidarity' they never let me in on in t'first place. Girls who did slitty eyes at me in science class, who've put on four stone since, asking how I can live with meself.

I tell 'em: this is what working class jobs used to be. Flexible, paid overtime. We're a growth industry: us, and prisons. Not my fault you ant kept up with modernity.

The ones that proper piss me off are them who make out they're fighting The Man by spunking someone else's money on a massive flat screen TV. This one sack of lard last week, clearly spent the entire loan on KFC cos she were visible from space – they tried to land that Rosetta satellite on her while I were there, swear to God – she kept going on about how I were a 'traitor to the working class'. Normally I try to stay, what's the word? Dispassionate. Keep a professional distance.

But this one deserved a little something.

So as we were serving the papers, I leant in and said, 'What d'you know about working class? You've never had either in your life.'

That shut her up.

The bottom line is: if you can't afford to pay a loan back, don't take it out.

Don't stand there quoting me figures, 'I only took out this much and you lot want three times as much back.'

Yes thank you Stephen Hawking, I can do the maths as well, the interest rate is down there in black and white.

Learn some discipline. If you ant got the money, do without.

I have. I *do*.

Lights down on **Denise**. *Lights back on* **Stefano**.

Stefano   My father was a fisherman. And his father before him. And before and before. I always thought, always knew, I'd make my living at sea.

But the fish are gone. The Med is dead.
And my job is to fish out a very different harvest.

Three years without work. Three years of pleading and queuing and niggly little bribes to a man who says he can help. And you sit, and you wait, and nothing happens, and you go back to him and he looks at you and shrugs and laughs a wheezy smoky laugh, and he doesn't give you your bribe back.

And you start again, your aims sinking slow like a pinholed boat. Turned down for stuff you turned your nose up at before. Borrowing money from my dad. Chiara's mum, who she doesn't get on with at the best of times.

And finally this. The job no-one else will take.

Beat.

I fucking wish they'd stop coming.

Not in the way Salvatore does.
Salvo's problem is he's an idealist. He joined to rescue
people. To 'help'.
Those people are always the most selfish because it's to help
on their terms.
And rescuing people is not the key part of the job. The key
to the job is the dead. And Salvo began very quickly to hate
these dead people, because they kept coming and coming
and they wouldn't stop.
He began to take it personally, like they were dying just to
upset him, to make him feel like a failure.
And now he calls them 'the niggers' and is going to vote
Berlusconi in the next election.
Ridiculous.
For one thing, Berlusconi is banned from the next election.
Read the papers you twat.
And for another, because they aren't.
Only.
Black.

Syrians are the latest thing. Palestinians last summer when
Gaza got bombed.
Egyptians and Libyans the past couple of years. We read the
papers and we see a disaster, a crackdown, a famine, and we
say: 'They'll be here next.'
Makes me laugh when people call them 'economic migrants'.
It's like an earthquake – you feel the tremors far away and
you know the tidal wave is coming.

My beef is why us?
This is a small island. The refugee centre is swamped, twelve
hundred in a place built for two or three. People sprawled
on blankets in the street, kids playing in the dust behind
barbed wire. It's embarrassing. Looks like Guantanamo.
We're a hospitable people but that centre makes us look
cruel and closed. But where else can we put 'em? And then a

chicken goes missing or some washing off a line, and there's shouting and we're the ones who look ignorant and small-minded, but where is everybody else? Why are we, a little dusty island you've never heard of, left to deal with all this alone?

And do the migrants not understand Europe is fucked? And Italy is double-fucked? And the south of Italy is triple-fucked? My younger brother, much smarter than me, degree in biochemistry (I think), and he had to go to London to find work . . . as a chef. He says the sous-chef is a biologist from Spain and the kitchen porter is a geneticist from Greece, and in their free time between courses they work on a cure for cancer.

It's a joke.
They don't get any free time.

Beat.

In Italy there's no hope. Everything is corrupt, the middle-aged cling grimly to their jobs and suffocate the young, and nobody has any idea how to fix it. Pessimism is our national sport, you can see it in our football.

And these people, the survivors, the lucky ones, they come on land with these shining, gleaming eyes. And I resent them for it. I'll be honest, I do.

I resent them for their hope.

Lights down on **Stefano**. *Lights up on* **Denise** *holding an essay.*

Denise   Spat at on the bus this morning.
Couple of public schoolboys, I'd say.
I'd not heard 'chinky cunt' and 'fucking migrant' in that accent till recently. But lately I get it quite a bit. Middle class people think racism is free speech now. Tip of the iceberg, Farage. Tip of a greasy gin-soaked iceberg of cuntery. The matchless bitterness of the affluent.

Summat about the Chinese an' all. We're the last ones it's OK
to hate. The last who you can take the piss out of to us faces,
cos we'll do nowt back and all we're good for is DVD sellers
and takeaway owners and whores. You can say stuff to the
Chinese you wouldn't even say to Muslims. And I'm not even
a proper one. Don't fit in anywhere, me. Old and mixed and
mouthy and poor.

Beat.

Here's something I found out the other day: nine out of the
ten poorest regions in Northern Europe, in comparative
terms, are in 'Great' Britain.

Would you like to know where they are?
West Wales
Cornwall
Tees Valley
Lincolnshire
The Independent Republic of South Yorkshire
Shropshire/Staffordshire
Lancashire
Northern Ireland
That's the top eight. Ninth is some wankstain in Belgium.
Tenth is East Yorkshire.

We also have one entry in the list of the ten richest areas.
It's the top entry, as it happens.
Can you guess where it is? I bet you'll never guess.
Inner London.

Put all that in me politics essay. It's why I do that job, to pay
for me degree. Got the grade today. C+. 'Too on the nose. A
lack of balance.' These are government figures. Nobody else
had them figures in their work, I checked. The prospectus
for this university claims to encourage original thinking.
Do you want the truth, or don't yer?

I used to read that prospectus obsessively, when Mam first
got sick and I had to drop out of me original course to look

after her. I'd read it, and look at her watching Jeremy Kyle, and be determined to do something with my mind.

Beat.

I can't stand this country now.

The hatred.

The hatred and the bitterness and the rage. The misplaced, thick, ignorant rage.

The endless waiting like sheep to the slaughter when the buses and trains, things you paid through the nose for, don't turn up. Ah well, mustn't grumble. Keep calm and carry on.

And the pushing and shoving and whining and grabbing when Black Friday rolls around. Me me me. Want want want.

Blaming 'fucking migrants' for every single thing we don't like about ourselves.

Four o'clock this afternoon, soaked to the skin, I'd been up and down more piss-stained staircases than a Channel 4 benefits documentary, and I banged on another door and yet another snide little prick yawned in me face, and kicked aside a knee-high pile of takeaway cartons, and spat at me when I asked him to pay, like I was the one in the wrong. And he did not have a Syrian or a Romanian or a Ugandan accent, let me tell you that.

Migrants don't hide their taxes in the Cayman Islands.
Migrants don't privatise the NHS.
And migrants don't scrape together their life savings, leave their loved ones behind, bribe and fight and struggle their way onto the undercarriage of a train or into a tiny hidden compartment of a lorry with forty other people, watch their mates die or get raped, all for the express purpose of blagging sixty-seven pound forty-six pence a week off of Kirklees District Council.
People just don't act like that.

And if you need to believe they do, what does that say about *you*?

Beat.

It don't matter.
What anybody says.
How many times me bloody mother tells me I'm too thick to pass.

I am going to murder these exams.
I'm going to Pistorius them, as I like to call it.
And if the results are good enough, I can go anywhere.
Australia. America.
China even. Doing well, ent they? That'd be fucking ironic.

Anywhere but here.

Slam the door on this bitter washed up country, turn me back, be *free*. I don't know what free is, where I'll find it, but that is where am I going and nobody will stop me.

Lights down on **Denise**. *Lights up on* **Stefano**.

Stefano   Boat wouldn't start last week.
Dawn. Beautiful morning, not a whisper on the water, the rocks dusted with peach and apricot. The breeze like a sigh of happiness.
And the boat won't start.

Not a soul around to help. Salvo and I fiddle with the engine for half an hour, no joy. We're on the point of chucking it in, when one of the mounds of rags piled up on the pier starts to stir and yawn.
Stocky, wine-dark skin.
Nigerian, my guess.
I've got decent at telling the difference between Eritreans, Somalis, Senegalese. I take a bit of pride in it, as it goes. We have bets on who's what and I've won a few drinks off it.

What?
This is all new to us.

He watches us struggling and cursing for a while, this lad, with a look of amusement on his face. Doesn't do anything to help. In the end Salvo storms off, lobs a few choice words in the fella's direction. Short pause, he gets up. I'm thinking he's gonna wake up his mates to come and watch.
And then he fixes the boat.
Five minutes, it took him. 'Easy for me,' he says, grinning.

Modibo. From Mali.
A mechanic.

Not much use for a boat mechanic in the Sahara, I tell him.
'Yes! This is why Europe needs me! Boats, cars, planes, all I can do!' he goes, massive smile all over his face.
'You want drink coffee?'
You want me to buy you a coffee?!
'No, I buy for you!' Big laugh this time.
I'm off to work, mate.
He offers to get in the boat with me in case it packs up again.
No thanks. Chirpy fucker.

Beat.

You try to keep them at arm's length. If you let them get close, you never know what they might ask for. On the boat the survivors start talking to me, pleading their case, like I can do anything for them.
It's not part of my job to have to listen to their stories.
There's too many of them.
And it makes you think.
About the randomness of I get to walk these streets and he doesn't.
You start thinking about things like that, the ground becomes ocean under your feet.

And what if he does get in and we break down and he fixes it again and the bosses hear? That he can do stuff I can't do, for half the rate? You have to think about these things now. Here, in Europe, 2015. You have to watch yer back from every angle.

Beat.

So I thank the fella, shake his hand, bell Salvo and away we
go. He waves to us as we head off, like a big gormless lump.
I think that's the end of it.
Except the mad bastard clearly hasn't got the memo that we
aren't gonna be mates, cos I keep running into him and he
keeps being nice to me.

His big guileless face, open smile. What's he got to be so
happy about? Keeps on offering to buy me an espresso, like
he's made of money.
Be rude to say no.
Salvo sees us in the café, gives me a look, mutters something
about 'soft touch'. He's paying, you gobshite!

Speaks shit Italian, Modibo. I say, why come somewhere you
don't speak the language? He says I didn't come here, I
came to Europe, the language of Europe is English.
Then he says something to me in English. I didn't
understand it.
I tell him *vaffanculo*. He understands that alright.
See, your Italian's improving already.

He plays me something as well. A song called Lampedusa.
It's meant to be about all the people who've come here
seeking a better life.
The drowning and the terror.
The hope and the futures.
I don't know if I can hear all that in there personally, but it's
beautiful. Listen.

'Lampedusa' by Toumani Diabaté and Sidiki Diabaté plays.

That big gormless grin like nothing bad's ever happened to
him in his whole life. Which, it turns out, it has.
His village was burned down twice. Once by the military
because they said it was a stronghold of Islamic
fundamentalists, and once by Islamic fundamentalists
because they said it was a stronghold of the military.
The second time, they gave them an hour to get out, said

they'd kill anyone left behind. He stashed his family and headed here. To earn the money to start afresh.

I mean, this is his story, God knows how much of it is true. He could be making it all up.

Mali. Exotic.

Beat. The music fades. Lights down on **Stefano**. *Lights up on* **Denise**.

Denise   Me mam got the dreaded ATOS call today. You know ATOS? Course you do. They do them Work Capability Assessments, where they go to morgues, plane crashes, outbreaks of bubonic plague, and tell people they'll be fine, it's just a head cold, and by the way their benefits have been stopped.

Mam's been called a lot of things over the years. She's gone from 'retarded' to 'slow' to 'disabled' to 'differently abled'. Which makes it sound like progress. Funny though, she's not *tret* any better. Kicked from pillar to post all her life, no wonder she were such a fucking –

She's not any of them things, as it happens.
She just don't like people.
She particularly don't like foreigners, which (*Waves a hand over her face.*) she must've made an exception for at some time, though she's never explained why. Barely who.

Beat.

One of the walls of her heart is thicker than it should be. Causes high blood pressure, hypertension, dizzy spells. Collapses. There's no way she can work.
She's a proper case, not like most of these I deal with. What work can she do? Fifty-eight years old, sick, thick, thinks a CV is an old French car, not getting a corner office is she?

The thing about ATOS is they're easy to play. They work on a target matrix, very much like us – this is the plus side of working for a payday loan company, it gives you a real insight into British society – and so you just play the matrix. Play the spastic, basically. I know it sounds harsh but . . .

All you need to do, Mam, is be aware of *everything*.
All the innocent little things you do in everyday life, when
you go in the office they are watching like a hawk and they
will hold them against you.
Do you get up unaided?
Could you walk?
Then you're not physically impaired.

Did you respond straight away when they called your name?
Did you fill out the form by yourself?
You've not got mental problems.

They have hidden cameras in their offices so they can
analyse all this at their leisure.

Well dressed is bad – awareness of social norms.
Pets are bad – ability to care for others.
Hobbies are bad – ability to function socially.

And all these abilities mean only one thing: *you can work*.

They take all the little things people do to make a good
impression, the things we do to prove that we are human
beings, and they use them to fuck you. That's the cruelty, the
breathtaking cruelty of it.

To pass an ATOS assessment you have to be, or play, a
locked-in idiot with no social skills, no friends, nobody that's
ever loved them in the history of the world.
Iain Duncan Smith, basically.

She's flapping, panicking, says she can't catch her breath.
How'll she live without her money?
Stop flapping, I say.
It's them as don't know how the system works who need to
worry.

Beat.

Summat odd came out of it, as it happens.
I was at a client's flat, she'd been tricky to get hold of,
wriggles out of stuff, but finally I'd got hold of her, and Mam
kept ringing. It were right embarrassing actually.

Now most of the kind I deal with would turn that to their advantage, but this lass . . .
'You alright?' she says.
Fine thanks. Let's get back to the matter at hand.
'Would you like a cup of tea?'

Be rude to say no. Don't like to be rude unless it's earned.

She sits me down at her kitchen table and we talk.
It's the expression on her face. No agenda, just nice.
A nice person.

Carolina, her name is. Portuguese lass, on her own with a little kid. Jayden.
I don't like kids.
Think it's all about them, don't they?

We talk about this and that, but at the back of me mind I'm thinking 'What's your game? Are you trying to butter us up so I'll let you off your money?' Cos I can't do that.
But that face of hers. So pretty and open.
Guileless, would be the word.
She just seemed to like us.

In the end she invited me over for dinner. Tomorrow night.
She's making some Portuguese speciality with salt cod in it.
Sounds absolutely disgusting, to be honest, but . . .

I shouldn't really go. It's against policy and all that.
But I think she's a bit lonely.
Doesn't know that many people over here.
I think she could do with the company.

Lights down on **Denise**. *Lights up on* **Stefano** *smoking furiously, pacing.*

Stefano   Dead kids weigh fucking nothing.
That's what I've learned today.

You need a couple of men to haul an adult corpse out of the water but it only takes one arm to haul in a dead kid. Course, normally they've been in for a while, got waterlogged. This lot were barely in half an hour. We hardly needed the boat, could've waded out . . .

This morning, a migrant boat, unusually overloaded even by the standards of migrant boats, overturned almost within sight of Rabbit Beach. So far we're looking at north of 350 dead. Salvo and I personally recovered seventy-four corpses today. Mainly children. Children and women. They run women-only boats now, cos they weigh less and you can get more in and then in the middle of the ocean, the smugglers can stop the boat and say there's one more payment . . .

It's bad enough when they're twenty-five. When they're five . . .

He stops pacing, squats, rubs his face with his hands for several moments.

Last year the users of TripAdvisor voted Rabbit Beach the most beautiful beach in the world. It's called Rabbit Beach because we used to raise rabbits on it before the tourists came. We're not a poetic people. Between tourism and the immigrant game, supplying the refugee centre or working for the NGOs, a lot of people on this island are making a lot of money all of a sudden.

God forbid anything stop the tourist industry.

The Russians are probably back there already, pleased to get it all to themselves apart from the odd corpse. Our lot rushing to serve them cold drinks.
They don't give a flying fuck about anyone, do they, the Russians?
'This is my holiday. I earned it.'
Ugly bastards too. When they sunbathe, the men look like the drowned but fatter.

The fucking *numbers*. We pulled out *four times* as many dead last year as the year before. FOUR TIMES. More than three thousand corpses. And those are just the ones we *found*. But nothing changes. People keep pouring in, they run more boats than ever before, boats from Turkey and Lebanon and

Libya and Egypt, boats with no crews that are set on a course
to crash into Europe. Rescue guaranteed cos nobody wants a
shipwreck off their coastline, so the price of the ticket goes
up. Ingenious fuckers, the smugglers.

On the radio this morning, they said this is the biggest global
mass migration since the Second World War. And all we do is
let them drown.

I ask Sal what are we going to do.
'Drink,' he says, and marches off, big broad back to me,
shoulders hunched up around his ears.

Beat.

Modibo is standing on the pier, staring at the rows of bodies,
his face haunted. I can only guess what, *who*, he's thinking
of. I realise I've never seen him without a smile before.

He turns to me and, very quietly, he says that it's deliberate.
That our glorious leaders *want* the migrants to drown, as a
deterrent, a warning to others. They want them to see TV
footage of the bloated bodies and the rotted faces of those
who trod the watery way of death before them, so they'll
hesitate before they set foot in one of those rickety little
deathtraps.

And he says they do see – and they get in anyway. They
know what the dangers are, but they keep coming and
coming because, in his words, 'if those men in their offices
knew what we were coming from, they'd know we will never,
ever stop.'

Beat.

It's not fair. That's all I can say. For them to be in sight of
land, within touching distance of safety, and for the boat to
go down, feels so fucking unfair. Maybe it's no worse than
drowning in the middle of a blue desert and nobody knows
you're gone, maybe there's no difference at the end of the
day. I don't know.

All I can tell you is how I feel.

Lights down on **Stefano**. *Lights up on* **Denise**.

Denise   *Bacalau*, it's called.

The Portuguese salt cod thing. You have to soak it for
twenty-four hours before you make it, which I were right
touched by, that she'd gone to all that effort. Butter,
potatoes, onions, garlic, peppers, parsley, then on top of that
chopped olives and hard-boiled eggs!
She sticks a plateful in front of me and smiles, and I lift a
forkful to me mouth and you know what I'm thinking . . .
I'm from fucking *Leeds*, for fuck's sakes. This is not for me.

And it were delicious. It were absolutely delicious.

Two helpings and a bottle and a half of red later and we're
gassing. Men, kids, jobs, family, the lot. She's not got a
remarkable story, but it's not the remarkable stories that
move you, is it?
Came over here to study English, met a fella, decided to stay,
had Jayden, the fella fucked off. Why do men do that? It's
like they live in a haze.
The thing about Carolina is she's not got an ounce of self-
pity. She's right in the middle of telling me about her
paediatric studies, I can't spell the word and she's studying it
in a foreign language so fair play, and how the fees have
gone way up and childcare is 'so fucking expensive in this
country' – I love the way she says 'fucking' with that little
growl, it's quite sexy actually – and so she's got behind with
the rent and she's had to go to this arsehole company for
money . . .

And we've both totally forgotten that's why I'm here.

And there's an excruciating pause, and then she laughs, and
I laugh, and she pours another glass of wine.

And so I tell her how to cancel the CPA we put on her
account. Send a letter to her bank by registered post, five
working days before payment is due, and we can't touch her.

People are remarkably ignorant of their rights in this country. The ones they still have.

Well. Least you can do when someone makes you dinner, ent it?

The touching thing is she's so bloody grateful. It's only a few months' breathing space but it seems to mean the world to her. Her fridge died last week. Jayden needs new shoes.

I don't make friends easily.
I'm not a giver. A confider. I cling on to what I am, my sense of self, like grim death, white bloody knuckles, because I've had to fight so bloody hard for every last inch of it.

But tonight I feel something shift inside me.
And then the phone rings.

Lights down on **Denise**. *Lights up on* **Stefano**.

Stefano I've not been able to sleep much.
Lot of nightmares.

The rotten fingers of the drowned clutching at my neck.
Grey faces of the long dead staring up from the seabed.
People I'd forgotten I'd fished out sitting on the end of the bed, glaring at me, seawater pooling on the sheets. They never speak, but the briny carrion stink of them . . .
Staring at me as if somehow I've betrayed them.

I swear I've woken up more than once because of the smell.
Open all the windows, turn the lights on. Nothing there, obviously.

Chiara understands but she doesn't understand, you know? We have a deal. Don't bring your work home with you. Which is fair enough. And after a few nights she's starting to get pissed off. I've tried the sofa but the noise, well I don't believe I make any noise, but the kids come in frightened and Daddy's fine, he's fine, go back to bed . . .

Beat.

Difficult to speak to anyone. Salvo would use it to get at me, hide his own fears and worries. We're fishermen and fishermen die. You're not supposed to make a big deal of death, you mourn and you get back to life while you've still got it. But there's never been a time when three hundred and fifty have died at once. In sight of shore. With no-one to mourn for them.

Which is why the only one who understands is Modibo.

He doesn't ask me about it, he just listens. He understands, not the words sometimes but the gist. They've all *seen* it, been through it, know people who've not survived.
They know what's really happening.

He got temporary leave to remain.
I guess his story checks out, though God knows how they make these decisions anyway.
The light of joy in his face when he found out. The pure unadulterated joy. Jumping and hugging with his mates and the happiness on their faces too, when half of them won't get what he's got and'll get sent back and they all know that, but they were really genuinely happy for him. Fucking lifts your heart.

It's been bloody good for me to be around him, actually. He's been a real mate.

So I've decided to be a good mate back.

Lights down on **Stefano**. *Lights up on* **Denise**.

Denise   I try not to go. I tell Carolina it's just me Mam, this is what she's like. Attention-seeking. It won't be serious. Bit of asthma. But she insists. 'It's your mother. Of course I'll drive you.'

I hate going over there. The state of the place.
The grime between the bathroom tiles.
The ring of encrusted shit around the toilet.
The memories of boredom and terror.

In the whole flat there's not a single book. How is that even possible? Not a book, not a picture, not a piece of culture in the whole house, never has been. Nothing to connect her to the rest of the human race. No food in the fridge. And it'd be fine if Mam were happy with that, but she hates it. All she ever does is moan.

It scares the shit out of me. It fucking terrifies me that I could end up like that, like a dried fly in a web the spider forgot to eat. It's what keeps me going, keeps me pressing . . .

There's no reason for me to feel guilty. She doesn't like me, never has. But we go over and I see *my* mam lying on the floor, gasping for air, in the midst of all this squalor, and nobody gives a toss and I'm the one that supposed to. And then Carolina steps through the door, and the look she gives me when she sees the state Mam's living in . . .

A *flood* of shame. You see the mildewed curtains and peeling ceilings in a whole new light then.

Paramedics are very quick. They say it were probably down to stress on top of her existing condition. Does she have anything in particular worrying her? Anything that might have stressed her out at all?

Beat.

It's a heart attack.

Lights down on **Denise**. *Lights up on* **Stefano**.

Stefano   He's sent for Aminata.
His wife.
He says if he's going to be here that long, he can't stand to be without her.
Which means she's got to come in by the same route.

The most terrifying bit for the families of migrants, and I'd never even thought about this, is that when they undertake the crossing itself they're completely out of contact. The rest of the way they've got phones, they can keep in touch, but when they enter the Blue Desert they disappear. Sitting there, staring at your phone, wondering if the person you love is ever going to ring it ever again.

Beat.

Aminata's boat left Libya yesterday morning. It's a thirty-six hour journey on average, depending on the engine and if the boat's only overloaded or fucking overloaded. But if the weather's rough, and the forecast is brutal, it can take days.

Days of staring at his phone. Wondering if it'll ever ring again.

I volunteered to take the boat out tonight and try and find her. I'll tell Salvo there's been an alert.

Beat.

The look on Modibo's face when I told him. Almost broke my heart.

He gave me a photo of her and told me to take care. To come back safe.
Both of us.

Lights down on **Stefano**. *Lights up on* **Denise**.

Denise   They turf Mam out of hospital a few days later. The nurses, who are *lovely*, want to keep her in for another week, but the consultant, who's a shiny-haired *cunt*, mutters 'bed blockers' and saunters off. I shout after him, 'Are bed blockers not the same as sick people?', but he doesn't stop, urgent golf course to attend to. So out she goes.

Pitiful state, can barely hobble to the bus stop. Naturally she doesn't want my help, snaps at me if I try to hold her arm. I watch her stagger and wheeze through the puddles in the car park, almost on hands and knees, and I think, 'Come on then ATOS, have a look at this and call her fit for work.' And I laugh out loud.

I don't even coach her for her interview. Piece of piss. 'You just go in there, Mam, and be your natural warm and vibrant self, and we will be just fine.'

Watch her dress in the same old shabby shit she's been wearing for donkey's years, take a full ninety-two seconds to hobble from waiting room to office, drool slightly onto her forms, and I'm thinking   we've got no problem here. And when the bastard shifts slightly in his seat and starts throwing the odd question my way, not many, no alarm bells go off. I know how to handle them.

Beat.

It's me.
That's their excuse.

I 'provide her with sufficient support structure to facilitate a return to paid employment.' Without me she'd get the fifteen points you need for Employment Support Allowance, but given my 'obvious capacity to compensate for the applicant's own shortcomings . . .'

This woman I've spent my whole life trying to get away from, they're tethering me to her. Till the day she dies.

I go mad. Three days solid on the phone arguing she meets Exceptional Circumstances under Regulation 25, she's limited capacity for work-related activity, Regulation 31.

They *hate* that. They blank me and block me and fob me off, tens of thousands of pounds in man hours to deny us this pitifully, embarrassingly small sum of money, and I keep pushing and pushing, and I hear the vitriol in their voices.

But I win. I fight and scratch and play them at their own game till in the end they refer the case to an appeals tribunal. The set-up there is still rigged, but they've gotta be a bit more public about it, which gives you a chance.

I prepare meticulously.
Go through all the documentation.
Get Mam ready. No stone unturned this time.
Go over me speech time after time.

The tribunal is this Thursday.

Lights down on **Denise**. *Lights up on* **Stefano** *soaking wet, totally drenched.*

Stefano   It's still at first, but right from the off you can tell it's coming. Salvo muttering that he didn't get an alert and staring up at the sky. In the dark we can't see the black clouds building up, but we can feel them. Sticky. Static.

Then the wind picks up, and the waves start to lift the boat and dump it back down again. You can tell how much trouble you're in at sea by how hard the boat thumps down between swells, and we're hitting the water harder and harder. Water is rock hard when you hit it like that. Your fillings jar in your mouth. Rain thrashes on the windscreen. Something shatters on the console.

The pauses at the top of the swells get longer and longer, huge waves loom out of the dark like sea monsters, and then the sickening lurch down into the trough and the THUMP vibrating through your guts and bones. Sal is screaming at me, screaming at the top of his lungs and I can still barely hear him, that this is insane and he's turning us back when suddenly, not far away, in between giant swells, I spot a light. Low in the water, pitching and yawing, obviously in big trouble.

A migrant boat.

I scream at Sal to head towards it and he doesn't want to, you can see he's afraid for us but what kind of coastguard, what kind of man, leaves a boat to go down? We swing around, which means we're perpendicular to the waves, they're crashing across us, drenching us, and that is when you can go under. I'm raging at Sal, veins popping, throat raw, to get us back in line, get us back in line, when there's a flash of lightning and out of the corner of my eye, this Leviathan looms. A monstrous wave as tall as a tower block, so tall it has little waterfalls tumbling from its crest.

I freeze. And Sal freezes. And Leviathan pounces.

A roar, and it slams us under its paw, and the whole boat goes under. The monster presses us down down down into the depths, and I breathe salt water and I don't know whether to cling onto the boat or let it sink and take my chances, and I realise it doesn't matter.
It doesn't matter what I do.

Beat.

And then, for some reason, for no *reason*, the boat squirms free and we pop out onto the surface, gasping and choking, the roar of the storm louder than ever. I look at Sal and he's pale as death, pale as one of the drowned. We're heading into the teeth of the storm, every time we climb one of the waves I don't think we're gonna reach the top, but we do and we're getting there. We're getting closer and closer to the light, maybe a couple of hundred metres at most. And then, all of a sudden, it goes out. The light vanishes.

Sal hunches over the wheel and his knuckles whiten even more and he kicks out at the boat, screaming at it, pick the fuck up you fuck, you fuck, you fucker, but all that picks up is the wind. The storm holds us at arm's length, watching us squirm and strive, laughing at us, refusing to let us get any closer. For half an hour we make no headway.

And then all of a sudden the wind drops. And the noises start.

Beat.

A loud thump against the hull.
A pause.
And then another thump, and then another, and another.

Most of the equipment is broken or gone but one of the terawatt lights is still intact, and I don't want to turn it on, please don't make me turn it on, but I turn it on and in the conical glare of light we see them coming, the storm mockingly pushing them towards us.

The black silhouettes of corpses.

Dozens of corpses are floating in the water around us.
Thumps against the hull coming in twos and threes. I grab
the first body I can, wrench it halfway aboard, turn it over,
and . . .

It's got Modibo's face.

I don't mean the body *looks* like Modibo, he *is* Modibo. He's
got my friend's face, but dead and gone.

I scream in pure terror and drop the body back in the
ocean. Sal staring at me like I've lost my mind. I lean back
against the side and howl like a child. Sal shakes me, slaps
me across the face. 'You fucking brought us out here. You do
your fucking job. Get them in.' I pull myself up, lean over
the side, drag another one in, flip him over, and . . .

He's got Modibo's face.
Every one of the fifty-seven bodies I recovered that night
had Modibo's face.

And I keep pulling them in. If I can't bring her back alive, at
least I can bring her back.

Lights down on **Stefano**. *Lights up on* **Denise**, *holding a
small urn.*

Denise　Mam died the night before the tribunal. Massive
coronary. Instantaneous.

There'll be an inquest but the paramedic, same fella as the
time before, very kind, he said it's almost impossible to tell.
If the worry killed her, or it would've happened anyway with
her condition.

But I know.

Beat.

There were three people at the funeral.
The priest.
The fella who presses the button to send the stiff down into

the fiery furnace. Who was chewing gum and staring out the
window the entire time. Commitment to excellence.
And me.

And then it were five.
Carolina and Jayden turned up. Poor little bugger. Top day
out for him.

Why are people kind?
It's the most unlikely thing.

I couldn't cry at first. You feel obliged to cry. But I couldn't.
Till she turned up.
Tears from kindness. Just leaked out.

(*Indicates urn.*) I think I'll take her ashes up the moors on a
windy day. Mam hated walking, absolutely loathed it. Exactly
where she wouldn't want to be.

Scatter them far and wide. As far away as possible.
Bye Mam.

Been telling meself that for a while now.
Still got 'em, though. For some reason.
I've wanted to be unyoked from you for so long, and now it's
happened I . . .

Beat.

I go back to work straight after the funeral. Uni won't let me
graduate if I don't pay the fees. Cuts are biting, loans are
rising. Plenty of work. They say it's a 'recovery' but it's not a
fucking recovery in Beeston, let me tell you that.

But suddenly all their flats look like Mam's.
The same streaks of filth on the walls. The same worn-
through carpet with the underlay showing. The same sense
of hopelessness and helplessness.

And then the other day something proper mad happens.
I'm collecting off this old lady and she's in floods, which is
obviously hard but after a while you get a bit hardened to it,
you think maybe they're turning the waterworks on for your

benefit, though this one seemed genuine enough.
Eventually she stops crying and turns to reach into her
handbag, and when she turns back, she has Mam's face.
Her dead grey stare, full of reproach.

Fucking hell.

I give the old dear another week and sprint out the door,
down the stairs, can't wait for the lift, flight after flight of
stairs, she lives on the fourteenth floor, and behind me her
tearful voice echoing down the stairwell, calling out in
gratitude.

Beat.

I quit the job that afternoon.
Packed it in. I just fucking couldn't any more, you know?

Lights down on **Denise**. *Lights up on* **Stefano**.

Stefano   We found her.

It took all night but we found her.

There were only three people pulled alive out of the sea that
night, and Aminata was one of them.

We travel back in the breaking dawn. Grey turning orange
turning blue. Five live bodies and fifty-seven dead ones.
Nobody says a word, each ocean-deep in their own thoughts.
Sal kicks me and nods at Aminata and says, 'Is it her? Is that
why we came?' And I nod.

'I have a son,' is all he says to me. 'A *son*.'
He hunches over the wheel. No more words till we reach
land.

We pull up to the pier. It's packed, a wall of people, and I'm
scanning for Modibo's face but there's a splash, Aminata's
over the side and into the shallows, and there's a kind of
keening noise from the pier and a second splash and it's
him, he's in the water too! These two torpedoes rocketing
together, to meet in an explosion of sheer joy and relief and

the ecstasy of deepest pain averted. Limbs entangled, rolling over, yelling, laughing, water splashing everywhere, this fantastical new sea creature. Tears and hands over mouths and hugging on the pier. Even Salvo's got tears in his eyes, the old cynic, though he's trying to hide them. I tell him thanks. He turns away, but he hears me.

I have never seen two happier people in all my born days.

Me? I still have fifty-seven bodies to unload.

Lights down on **Stefano**. *Lights up on* **Denise** *holding an envelope.*

Denise   I don't go out for a couple of days. Even though it's finals lectures and I am *so far* behind. I can't fail now, not after all I've done.

A knock on the door.
Carolina.
'You're not answering your phone.'
Yeah, no, I'm fine.
A pause. I think she's gone away. A lurch in me chest. And then she says,
'Listen, you might think it's crazy, but will you move in with us?'
What? What you talking about?
'The couch folds out. If we split the rent I can start to pay my loan. And maybe you can quit your job.'
A silence. Is this a joke?
'I trust you,' she says.
'I don't trust easily but I trust you. I don't know why.
Will you think about it?
Please?'

Beat.

Fucking hell. Fucking, fucking hell.
Why are people kind?

She's just brought me this. Delivered this morning.
Exam results.

The last question on me last exam was on the monkey trap. You know the one. Where the monkey can get its hand into the coconut shell to pull out treats but it can't pull out its fist with the treats still in them, so the villagers can catch it. The question was, 'What does this experiment suggest about the perils of untrammelled materialism?'

You could see the answer they wanted. This home of original thinking.

But the monkey trap's always meant summat different to me.
Cos I've never had the balls to put me hand in in t'first place. Never could admit there was anything I wanted, because I knew I couldn't have it and I'd only get hurt.

So I took a different tack.
I wrote that empirical studies of the monkey trap experiment do not support the presumed hypothesis of inherent greed. To wit: in the vast majority of test cases, the monkeys let go of the treats. They demonstrate a clear understanding of the relative importance of grated coconut vis-à-vis their own bollocks.

That's not me answer word for word, obviously.

I wrote that the monkey trap experiment is fundamentally an indicator of *hope*. It speaks to our ability to walk away from delusions, from traps. To save ourselves from our baser instincts.

Me last line, and I can't believe I actually wrote this hippy shit but fuck it, was, 'Perhaps the ultimate purpose of the experiment is for the monkeys to teach us something.'

She looks at the envelope. She wants to open it but she doesn't want to lose the pride of this moment. Lights stay up on **Denise**. *Lights come up on* **Stefano**.

Stefano   They had their second wedding today.
Their 'European wedding', they called it. To celebrate her coming back from the dead.

Chiara loaned her a dress, looked really good on her actually.

Nothing fancy, just a party in the camp.
Malian food and music.
Dancing and laughing and hugging and more dancing. I'm completely shattered.
Dragged Sal along, after much protest. He's still dancing.
Didn't think much of the food though.

I was the guest of honour. Imagine that. The bloody guest of honour.

They've given us joy.
And hope.
They've brought us the things we have nothing of.
And I thank them for that.

They don't know what'll happen. If either of them will get to stay long-term. But they're here, in this moment, alive and living. And that is all you can ask for.

I defy you to see the joy in Modibo and Aminata's faces and not feel hope.
I defy you.

Stefano *and* **Denise** *look warily at one another.*

'Lampedusa' starts to play.

Denise *holds on to the envelope.*

Blackout.

End of play

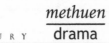

Bloomsbury Methuen Drama Modern Plays

include work by

Bola Agbaje	Robert Holman
Edward Albee	Caroline Horton
Davey Anderson	Terry Johnson
Jean Anouilh	Sarah Kane
John Arden	Barrie Keeffe
Peter Barnes	Doug Lucie
Sebastian Barry	Anders Lustgarten
Alistair Beaton	David Mamet
Brendan Behan	Patrick Marber
Edward Bond	Martin McDonagh
William Boyd	Arthur Miller
Bertolt Brecht	D. C. Moore
Howard Brenton	Tom Murphy
Amelia Bullmore	Phyllis Nagy
Anthony Burgess	Anthony Neilson
Leo Butler	Peter Nichols
Jim Cartwright	Joe Orton
Lolita Chakrabarti	Joe Penhall
Caryl Churchill	Luigi Pirandello
Lucinda Coxon	Stephen Poliakoff
Curious Directive	Lucy Prebble
Nick Darke	Peter Quilter
Shelagh Delaney	Mark Ravenhill
Ishy Din	Philip Ridley
Claire Dowie	Willy Russell
David Edgar	Jean-Paul Sartre
David Eldridge	Sam Shepard
Dario Fo	Martin Sherman
Michael Frayn	Wole Soyinka
John Godber	Simon Stephens
Paul Godfrey	Peter Straughan
James Graham	Kate Tempest
David Greig	Theatre Workshop
John Guare	Judy Upton
Mark Haddon	Timberlake Wertenbaker
Peter Handke	Roy Williams
David Harrower	Snoo Wilson
Jonathan Harvey	Frances Ya-Chu Cowhig
Iain Heggie	Benjamin Zephaniah

Bloomsbury Methuen Drama Contemporary Dramatists

include

John Arden (two volumes)
Arden & D'Arcy
Peter Barnes (three volumes)
Sebastian Barry
Mike Bartlett
Dermot Bolger
Edward Bond (eight volumes)
Howard Brenton (two volumes)
Leo Butler
Richard Cameron
Jim Cartwright
Caryl Churchill (two volumes)
Complicite
Sarah Daniels (two volumes)
Nick Darke
David Edgar (three volumes)
David Eldridge (two volumes)
Ben Elton
Per Olov Enquist
Dario Fo (two volumes)
Michael Frayn (four volumes)
John Godber (four volumes)
Paul Godfrey
James Graham
David Greig
John Guare
Lee Hall (two volumes)
Katori Hall
Peter Handke
Jonathan Harvey (two volumes)
Iain Heggie
Israel Horovitz
Declan Hughes
Terry Johnson (three volumes)
Sarah Kane
Barrie Keeffe
Bernard-Marie Koltès (two volumes)
Franz Xaver Kroetz
Kwame Kwei-Armah
David Lan
Bryony Lavery
Deborah Levy
Doug Lucie

David Mamet (four volumes)
Patrick Marber
Martin McDonagh
Duncan McLean
David Mercer (two volumes)
Anthony Minghella (two volumes)
Tom Murphy (six volumes)
Phyllis Nagy
Anthony Neilson (two volumes)
Peter Nichol (two volumes)
Philip Osment
Gary Owen
Louise Page
Stewart Parker (two volumes)
Joe Penhall (two volumes)
Stephen Poliakoff (three volumes)
David Rabe (two volumes)
Mark Ravenhill (three volumes)
Christina Reid
Philip Ridley (two volumes)
Willy Russell
Eric-Emmanuel Schmitt
Ntozake Shange
Sam Shepard (two volumes)
Martin Sherman (two volumes)
Christopher Shinn
Joshua Sobel
Wole Soyinka (two volumes)
Simon Stephens (three volumes)
Shelagh Stephenson
David Storey (three volumes)
C. P. Taylor
Sue Townsend
Judy Upton
Michel Vinaver (two volumes)
Arnold Wesker (two volumes)
Peter Whelan
Michael Wilcox
Roy Williams (four volumes)
David Williamson
Snoo Wilson (two volumes)
David Wood (two volumes)
Victoria Wood

For a complete listing of Bloomsbury
Methuen Drama titles, visit:

www.bloomsbury.com/drama

Follow us on Twitter and keep up to date
with our news and publications

@MethuenDrama